First World War
and Army of Occupation
War Diary
France, Belgium and Germany

25 DIVISION
74 Infantry Brigade,
Brigade Trench Mortar Battery
1 July 1916 - 31 August 1916

WO95/2247/6

The Naval & Military Press Ltd
www.nmarchive.com
Published in association with The National Archives

Published by

The Naval & Military Press Ltd

Unit 10 Ridgewood Industrial Park,

Uckfield, East Sussex,

TN22 5QE England

Tel: +44 (0) 1825 749494

www.naval-military-press.com

www.nmarchive.com

This diary has been reprinted in facsimile from the original. Any imperfections are inevitably reproduced and the quality may fall short of modern type and cartographic standards.

© Crown Copyright
Images reproduced by permission of The National Archives, London, England, 2015.

Contents

Document type	Place/Title	Date From	Date To
Heading	WO95/2247-7 74th Trench Mortar Bty Jul-Aug 1916		
Heading	74th Trench Mortar Bty Jly-Aug 1916		
Heading	74th Trench Mortar Battery.July 1916		
War Diary		01/07/1916	31/07/1916
Heading	74th Trench Mortar Battery August 1916		
War Diary		01/08/1916	31/08/1916

25TH DIVISION
74TH INFY BDE

74TH TRENCH MORTAR BTY
JLY-AUG 1916

74th Inf. Bde.

25th Division

74th TRENCH MORTAR BATTERY.

J U L Y,   1 9 1 6.

Army Form C.2118.

25
74 B M B
Vol. 1

WAR DIARY
or
INTELLIGENCE SUMMARY

(Erase heading not required.)

Instructions regarding War Diaries and Intelligence Summaries are contained in F.S. Regs., Part II. and the Staff Manual respectively. Title Pages will be prepared in manuscript.

Place	Date	Hour	Summary of Events and Information	Remarks and references to Appendices
	Saturday 1/7/16		Billets at Warloy.	
	Sunday 2nd		do.	
	Monday 3rd		Marched to billets at Bouzincourt.	
	Tuesday 4th		Billets at Bouzincourt.	
	Wednesday 5th		do.	
	Thursday 6th		Relieved the 57th T.M.B. in the trenches at La Boiselle.	
	Friday 7th		In the trenches at La Boiselle. Lieut P. Erskine 2nd R.I.R. was wounded & one other rank.	
	Saturday 8th		In action.	
	Sunday 9th		In action. Rifle grenading & mortars & ammunition up to new front line. 2nd Lieut H.G. Charles 9th K.V.L. was wounded.	
	Monday 10th		In action. Relieved in night by 7th T.M.B. in early morning & marched to Billets at Senlis. In billets at Senlis.	
	Tuesday 11th		do.	
	Wednesday 12th		do. 2nd Lieuts Bayton & Solly joined for duty from 11th L.F's.	
	Thursday 13th		In reserve in wood behind Ulsna Redoubt.	
	Friday 14th		Relieved the 7th T.M.B. in trenches round Guillers-la-Boiselle.	
	Saturday 15th		In the trenches & in action.	
	Sunday 16th		do.	
	Monday 17th		Relieved during morning by 143rd T.M.B. & marched to billets at Bresville.	
	Tuesday 18th		Marched to billets at Beauval.	
	Wednesday 19th		In billets at Beauval. Inspection by G.O.C. Division.	GAS
	Thursday 20th		do.	

Army Form C. 2118.

WAR DIARY
or
INTELLIGENCE SUMMARY
(Erase heading not required.)

Instructions regarding War Diaries and Intelligence Summaries are contained in F. S. Regs., Part II and the Staff Manual respectively. Title Pages will be prepared in manuscript.

Place	Date	Hour	Summary of Events and Information	Remarks and references to Appendices
Friday	21st		Marched to billets at Bus-les-Artois.	
Saturday	22nd		In billets at Bus. Work as per training programme.	
Sunday	23rd		do.	
Monday	24th		Relieved the 87th T.M.B. in trenches opposite Beaumont-Hamel. Ammunition cleaned & work on new emplacements commenced.	
Tuesday	25th			
Wednesday	26th		do. Work carried on.	
Thursday	27th		do. do.	
Friday	28th		do. do.	
Saturday	29th		do. do.	
Sunday	30th		do. do.	
Monday	31st		do. At 11 p.m. we carried out retaliation with 2 Stokes mortars on an enemy T.M. position, which had been annoying our posts. 240 rounds were got off & the guns got away from the positions, which were rather exposed, without any casualties.	

E. H. Steel, Capt.
O.C. 94th T.M.B.

31.7.16.

74th Inf. Bde.

25th Division.

74th TRENCH MORTAR BATTERY,

AUGUST, 1916.

Army Form C. 2118.

WAR DIARY
or
INTELLIGENCE SUMMARY
(Erase heading not required.)

Volume 1 2nd T.M. Batn. Diary
Part 1. August 16 VOL 2

Instructions regarding War Diaries and Intelligence Summaries are contained in F. S. Regs., Part II. and the Staff Manual respectively. Title Pages will be prepared in manuscript.

Place	Date	Hour	Summary of Events and Information	Remarks and references to Appendices
Tuesday	1.8.16		In trenches opposite Beaumont Hamel. Ammunition cleaned and works on Emplacements carried on.	
Wednesday	2.8.16		do.	
Thursday	3.8.16		do.	
Friday	4.8.16		do. and two Emplacements prepared at junction of Chaney Cross Road and Long Acre for Offensive measures.	
Saturday	5.8.16		do. Relieved by 71st T.M.B. Marched to billets in BEAUSSART.	
Sunday	6.8.16		In billets at BEAUSSART.	
Monday	7.8.16		Relieved 61st T.M.B. in trenches Q4b.6.6. to junction of Flag and Legend Street. One gun at the end of Rat Street fired 40 rounds during the night in retaliation to enemy's trench mortars. This action silenced the enemy.	
Tuesday	8.8.16		In trenches. New offensive emplacements commenced on Left sector. Ammunition cleaned.	
Wednesday	9.8.16		ditto	
Thursday	10.8.16		Relieved by 3rd Guards Brigade T.M.Battery. Marched to billets at BUS-LES-ARTOIS	
Friday	11.8.16		In billets at BUS-LES-ARTOIS. Work as in Training Programme. Capt Stead went sick.	
Saturday	12.8.16		do.	
Sunday	13.8.16		do.	

Army Form C. 2118.

WAR DIARY or INTELLIGENCE SUMMARY

(Erase heading not required.)

Colonel H. - T.M Battery
August 16

Instructions regarding War Diaries and Intelligence Summaries are contained in F.S. Regs., Part II. and the Staff Manual respectively. Title Pages will be prepared in manuscript.

Place	Date	Hour	Summary of Events and Information	Remarks and references to Appendices
Monday	14.8.16		In billets BUS-LES-ARTOIS Work as in training programme	
Tuesday	15.8.16		Moved to ACHEUX WOOD do	
Wednesday	16.8.16		In huts in ACHEUX WOOD. Training as per training programme.	
Thursday	17.8.16		do	
Friday	18.8.16		Moved to Billets in HEDAUVILLE	
Saturday	19.8.16		In billets at HEDAUVILLE.	
Sunday	20.8.16		Relieved 147th T.M Battery in trenches opposite THIEPVAL.	
Monday	21.8.16		In the trenches in action.	
Tuesday	22.8.16		do	
Wednesday	23.8.16		do	
Thursday	24.8.16		do	
Friday	25.8.16		do	
Saturday	26.8.16		Relieved by 146th T.M. Battery and moved to billets at Bouzincourt.	
Sunday	27.8.16		In billets at Bouzincourt.	
Monday	28.8.16		Relieved 145rd and 146th T.M. Battery in trenches beyond OVILLERS.	
Tuesday	29.8.16		In trenches in action.	
Wednesday	30.8.16		do , digging gun emplacements	
Thursday	31.8.16		do	

W.J. Bolby 2nd Lieut
for O.C. 74th Trench Mortar Battery
31st August, 1916

www.ingramcontent.com/pod-product-compliance
Lightning Source LLC
Chambersburg PA
CBHW081253170426
43191CB00037B/2146